PRAYER, FAITH, and GUTS

Determined To Make It!

MEMOIRS OF MOM

JANICE MARIE HUNT

XULON PRESS

Xulon Press
2301 Lucien Way #415
Maitland, FL 32751
407.339.4217
www.xulonpress.com

Unless otherwise indicated, Scripture quotations taken from the King James Version (KJV) – *public domain.*

Scripture quotations taken from the Living Bible (TLB). Copyright © 1971 by Tyndale House Foundation. Used by permission of Tyndale House Publishers Inc., Carol Stream, Illinois 60188. All rights reserved.

Printed in the United States of America.

Makeup by Sholanda Reed
Mom Photo by Ronnie Tillman

ISBN-13: 978-1-54565-809-3

With permission and blessings, this book is dedicated to my beloved parents, Artie Marie Hunt and the late Eddie June Hunt: without them, my conception would not have been possible.

Thank you Ma for allowing me to share some of your most personal experiences.

To The World You May Be One Person,
But To One Person You May Be The World.
                              -Author Unknown-

But blessed are your eyes, for they see: and your ears, for they hear. For verily I say unto you, That many prophets and righteous men have desired to see those things which ye see, and have not seen them; and to hear those things which ye hear, and have not heard them.

Matthew 13:16, 17 (KJV)

Acknowledgments

These integrated experiences are just a few from my mother's journey, told in her own words and carefully woven together by faith and family. This may cause you to ask yourself, what do you believe?

Mom would often say, "I come this far on three things, prayer, faith, and guts, determined to make it because I knew all the odds were against me."

Special thanks to my siblings, Jetaun, Tammie, and Eddie, for sharing recollections of our mom who gives us a reason to believe.

My son's Greg and Roderick and granddaughter Cherish (Angel Face or Cherish Bunny), who contributed with their support and perspective of who Grandma and Granny means to them: and to Melody, my newest granddaughter, who has yet to meet Mom in person; however, I'm sure they have already connected in the spirit.

"Don't forget about Bruce," a loyal, committed, and longtime friend to my family and me.

And to all of you that bought a dollar raffle ticket to help defray the cost for this project; you made us one-thousand dollars strong and the publishing of this book a reality. Thanks for your support.

And lastly, I wish to thank Xulon Press Publishing and the entire team for guiding this project from beginning to end.

Love and Prayers,
-Janice Marie Hunt-

TABLE OF CONTENTS

Foreword

Please make no mistake about it; this is not a text book of theology, nor is it about some new phenomenon of God. It's about me, a simple woman who loves and trusts God, and He loves me back.

I'm not a perfect person without flaws, but a changed person who God saved and filled with His Holy Spirit, continuing to grow and mature along the way. What a long way to come.

I have my daughter Jetaun to thank for always praying and interceding for her family to be saved, filled with the Holy Ghost, and to speak with tongues.

God told me that the seed I carried and nurtured would be my blessing. I didn't even know I was a nurturer; however, I've lived long enough to see that and more.

I'm sure there will be readers that question some of these occurrences and even say this is not possible. I can only speak of what I have seen, heard, and experienced.

God told me to say exactly what He said, no more and no less, and don't be intimidated with their eyes because He made them too.

To God be the glory for the things He has done and continues to do. Thank you all and God Bless.

-Artie Marie Hunt-

INTRODUCTION

"Prayer, Faith, and Guts Determined To Make It" is the story of Mom's ongoing journey and struggles with her identity, being fatherless, and feeling of not being accepted as she moved through life: always wondering, searching, asking, and hoping.

Her only resolve is her faith in God, whom she has never seen but who has proven to be faithful, true, and more than what she has ever seen or known.

As I sit and talk to Mom, there are so many dreams, visions, and revelations that God has shown her that are too numerous to mention all of them. Even during and after writing this book, the dreams, visions, revelations, and conversations continue.

Thank you all for taking this journey along with our family.

A Song Dedicated To Mom

When thinking of the lyrics "Lean On Me" by Melba Moore, I think of God talking to Mom about the journey her life was going to take and how He was going to be with her every step of the way.

Mom, here's to you.

Just let me walk
This road of life with you.
Step by step, uphill or down,
No matter where it's leading to.

Reach out and take my hand.
If you should find a hill along the way too steep to climb,

Lean on Me
I'll never let you fall
Lean on Me
I'll keep you standing tall

Moore, Melba. "Lean On Me."

www.metrolyrics.com/lean-on-me-lyrics-melba-moore.html.

12/31/2018

Album Title *"This Is It"*

Cobb, J., & McCoy, V. (Composers). (1976). Lean On Me. [M.
Moore, Performer] New York, New York, USA.

Label. Buddah Records

One

WHO AM I

ᠥᠥᠥ

W hat happened to a child with an unknown identity, born in 1940 in Mason, Tennessee to an unwed fifteen-year-old or younger mother and an unknown father? Who did she look like with those grey eyes and fair complexion, denied by a man who allegedly was her father?

She was embarrassed, ashamed, and alienated, even in the very house where she lived with her other eight siblings; always the child on the outside looking in and wanting to belong. How was this possible? Why was this happening to her? She didn't ask to be in this predicament, but what child did?

There was another sibling, James like her; they were close and he was an outcast for the same reason. James was sent to live with Grandma in Buffalo. His life didn't fare any better there, but that's another story.

Bullying didn't just start with today's social media; it was happening way back then. While at Bernard School, kids were just as cruel, name- calling her; "Hey grey eyes, cat eyes, who's your father?" They wrote on the blackboard, "Artie looks like she's got TB." During the high school commencement, one of the students said, "I'm going to will my brain to Artie." How humiliating. The principal once told her fellow class mates, "Artie will never have anything." They went back and told her.

Once mom was at the fair with some friends, and while there she recognized this man who she was told was her father. She told her friend, "That's my father." She shouldn't have said anything, and how she wished she hadn't. Her friend said; "Well, if he's your father, ask him for some money," and so she did.

She walked over to him and asked, "Dad, can I have some money?" He looked at her and said, "Little girl, I'm going to give you this money, but I am not your father." Man, talking about more humiliation for her.

Mom was always told that she wouldn't have anything but a house full of babies, a one-room shack, and Adel Neal a childhood boyfriend.

Thank God she didn't get what people thought she should have, and that God had plans for her life that went far above anything she could have imagined.

> Jeremiah 29:11 (TLB): "For I know the plans I have
> for you," says the Lord. "They are plans for good
> and not for evil, to give you a future and a hope."

Much later in life, Mom learned to look at scripture or a song where she always found meaning and comfort concerning the will of God for her life.

Two

LEARNING TO COUNT MONEY

I n the early 1970s, the Hunts had a delicatessen on the corner of French and Kehr in Buffalo, New York. Mom said those Negroes on French Street were something else, very uppity. Back in those days, all the neighborhood stores were owned and operated by black families.

The five Hunt brothers were no exception: they were running the store with their wives, girlfriends, and a whole lot of other folks that didn't need to be there, and that included my dad as well.

Everybody wanted a piece and many got some. Mom looked back at those times and laughed, but it was no laughing matter many days for her.

There had been talk about the young girls hanging around the store. Whew, child, you talking about a mess. You know, the store could have been successful, but there was way too much stuff going on.

During those days, many times one of the brothers had to go to the Sho Shon's Brother Warehouse to pick up merchandise for the store, but Mom couldn't be left alone because she could not count money. So someone would always have to stay at the store with her. This was every day.

After one of those longs days, on the way home, mom said my dad asked her, "What did you learn, today?" She felt so bad; her heart just sunk she was embarrassed and ashamed of not knowing how to count money. When they got home, Mom didn't stop walking. She went straight to the attic, sat on the stairs in the pitch black darkness, put her head in her hands, and began to cry.

When she looked up, there was a blackboard that flashed right before her. It stretched from one side of the room to the other, and on that blackboard there was money, beginning from dollars all the way down to pennies.

There was someone teaching her how to count money, give change, and weigh the food on the scale. In an instance, the blackboard disappeared as quickly as it had appeared.

The next day, it was time for Mom to put into action what she had been taught the night before. She was nervous, but ready. This particular day, a young lady was left with her in the store. One of her brother-in-laws asked before leaving, "Artie, are you going to be okay today?" She replied, "Yes, you can go; I am going to be okay."

Mom put some gum in her mouth to help steady her nerves, and like a lion waiting in the brush for its next opportunity to pounce on the prey, Mom waited for that first customer.

When that customer walked through those doors, Mom was like a lion let out of a cage. She took that money, gave back the change, and weighed the bologna on the scale.

Man, Mom and that young lady were working like a well-oiled machine. There were so many customers that day, and they made so much money that they didn't have time to put the money in the register. They were throwing the money on the floor and walking and stepping on it.

They made more money that day than had ever been made. No one ever had to stay with Mom again in the store, and she'd been counting money and making change ever since.

God truly is the world's greatest teacher, and He will bring all things to your remembrance. Hallelujah. Thank you Jesus. To God be the glory for real.

Three

MARCH 19, 1983

March 19, 1983 was the end of two lives that became one. However, several years prior to this date, mom recalls when my dad became ill the first time. We were living in the Fruitbelt at 262 Locust Street. He was still working as an NFTA bus driver, which he had been doing about nineteen or twenty years, and working in the store.

One particular day, a woman came into the store that happened to be a nurse. She noticed the white part of my dad's eyes were yellow. She told him, "You have jaundice, which is contagious, and you shouldn't be working." Mom didn't know what that was, how he got it, and she didn't ask any questions. Mom just knew her husband was sick.

Dad was off work for a very long time. He was already a man of small frame, and he had lost a considerable amount of weight. We received a lot of love and support from family and the customers, as everybody was wishing him well.

He eventually got better and then they lost the store. It was bound to happen with Dad being sick. My mom and dad were stuck paying the IRS and all the other bill collectors while dad's brothers went on. Mom said, "Money was short and none of those other Negroes could not be found, ooh child. Thank God for NFTA."

One day, my dad came home and told Mom he had been looking at this cute little house on Colorado Avenue. He liked nice things and he always desired to have a home of his own.

Mom said she recalls when Dad took her to see this house. It seemed so far away from where we lived. It was like another world, and it was. It definitely was more white folks than they had seen in a long time, but it was a very nice neighborhood. Mom remembered saying to him, "Why did you bring me over to this no man's land to die by myself? There aren't even any houses on the other side of the street."

Little did Mom know what she was saying.

There was this brick house on Moselle Street. It was nice; ooh Mom wanted that house so bad she could taste it, but boy, she often said, "I am so glad that your father didn't buy that house. God knew the plans all along."

Eventually, our family moved from the Fruitbelt and settled into the cute little house that later became our home.

It has three bedrooms, a bath and a half-bath, and all the other little rooms that make up a house. There is a nice sized backyard where there are so many fond memories of cookouts and parties.

It was just the right fit for our family. At the time, there were only two children, Janice (me) and my sister Jetaun. Mom didn't want any more children, but she often said God knew the plans.

Once in the middle of the night, while Mom and Dad were sleeping in one of the bedrooms upstairs, Mom said she got up and went to the bathroom when she saw this little girl at the bottom of the stairs looking up at her.

She was a cute little girl with sandy-colored hair; she never said anything, just looked at her. Mom didn't know how long this went on, but every time she would get up in the middle of the night and go to the bathroom, she would see her.

Now, on the other hand, my dad was scary with this news. Mom said she remembered saying to him, "Eddie, there is a little girl at the bottom of the stairs. I see her every time I go to the bathroom." His scared self asked, "What does she want?" Mom replied, "I don't know."

Well, not long after telling Dad, she didn't see this little girl anymore. Months later, Mom found out she was pregnant and when she awakened from the slumber of anesthesia after the birth, she was presented with this cute, little baby girl that she saw nightly at the bottom of the stairs. She is my sister Tammie. Mom conceived for the last time and had her one and only son, Eddie Craig; now our family was complete.

Times were good on Colorado. We had a great street! Neighbors looked out for each other, we had block parties, and everybody knew one another.

The kids played in the middle of the street or in our backyards. There were many families and childhood friends that made a difference in our lives; there was a real sense of community.

Darkness came on us on March 19, 1983, and this time my dad didn't get better. This would be the last time we saw him in Buffalo General Hospital. Mom went to visit him like she always did; "I waited for you," he told her when she arrived. She had no idea he was dying.

Mom said he shared a lot of personal things with her and then she witnessed his color changing and him having difficulty breathing. She told him "Honey, breathe through your mouth." She put the oxygen mask on him, but it didn't help. The doctors came in the room and asked her to step out, and then he was gone.

There was Mom all alone, a widow at forty-two years old and left with four children. I was twenty-two, Jetaun was seventeen, Tammie was ten, and Eddie was three.

Mom said she cried many days and asking God to make her house a home, not just a place where people came in from the elements. Little did she know that God had to remove my dad for that to happen.

After the dust had settled and the smoke had cleared, God began speaking to Mom and He hasn't stopped.

God told Mom that she had nothing but junk around her. Imagine that; she said, "No, I don't; I have family and friends." He said, "I am going to separate the wheat from the tare." Mom had no idea what God was talking about and that's when her journey began.

One of the many things God instructed Mom to do was get a composition book and to begin writing down all of her bills, taking the total of everything that came in and subtracting that from the money (the social security check) she was receiving. Can you believe it? God was still teaching and instructed her on how to handle her business since the death of her husband.

Mom often speaks of being grateful to God about how her life turned out. You can't even imagine how truly grateful she is. There was no one to help her navigate through the grieving process or assist with her children. She didn't want anyone to know what she didn't know about the practical or legal things to do in the death of her husband or even what to expect next.

God spoke these words to her: "I am the world's greatest teacher and I will teach you all things and bring all things to your remembrance. Touch not my anointed one and do my prophet no harm; you don't belong to yourself and I don't want you corrupted by man."

Mom asked God, "Where is the prophet? Are you talking about me?"

Four

WEDNESDAY PRAYER

One of our aunts once told Mom that her family had prayer once a month. She suggested that we should do the same as a family. Mom asked her, "Is that why your family is so blessed?" So Mom decided that our family would start having prayer every Wednesday at six o'clock.

We began having prayer in the living room of our home. Everyone was anointed with oil; we had to read a scripture or something inspirational; and then we would have open discussion about how our day was or what was going in our lives.

After the open discussions, we'd stand in a circle, close with prayer, and then hugged and tell each other "I love you." This continued for many years.

On this particular night, as we prepared to close with prayer, Mom's grandson Roderick asked if he could pray. He was very young, and he could barely talk.

When he began to pray, Mom said she looked at him and noticed his countenance had changed. The last thing he asked God to do was to bless Tammie with her new "yob." He couldn't pronounce job. God not only heard that request, but He also answered it. Tammie has been with her new "yob" for sixteen years.

Five

THE FURRY BEARS

S everal years ago, Janice (me) was selected as a juror on a murder trial. We won't mention the case by name. Now, you're probably wondering what does this have to do with anything, especially God and faith? A lot, so let's begin.

The trial was about a rivalry between two biker gangs that lasted several months. The phrase "furry bears" was given because of their appearance: white males, the burly-type, like mountain men, with bushy beards and tinted sunglasses. The trial ended finding the accuser innocent and that's when things begin to happen.

It wasn't noticed right away, but Mom was being followed everywhere and threatened by these "furry bears." Now, you're probably wondering, "Why would they be following her? She wasn't one of the jurors." That is the same thing we all were thinking, but they were. It was the most frightening and eerie experience our family ever had.

Once while Mom was shopping for some shoes at DSW in the Northtown Plaza, along came this "furry bear." Mom said he looked about three hundred to four hundred pounds. He stood right next to her and whispered, "We know you're going up north, but we're still going to kill you." Mom was so scared that she hurried up and put those shoes back and left the store.

Mom would be driving anywhere and look in her rearview mirror and see them following her.

One year, Mom went to Tennessee to visit her parents and they followed her there. Now, she wasn't certain if they were the same ones from Buffalo, but they sure had strong resemblances.

When Miss Ruth a neighbor picked Mom up from the airport, Mom immediately noticed they were being followed. Miss Ruth kept looking in her rearview mirror with a puzzled and concerned expression on her face; Mom didn't dare say a word. As they got further away from Memphis and turned down 59 Highway, Miss Ruth let the hammer down and they sped away in that Cadillac. The furry bears were no longer in sight.

Shortly after Mom arrived at her parents' home, the telephone rang. The voice on the other end asked, "How many people are in the house?" She responded fifteen and hung up the phone.

Mom said she could detect their presence anywhere she was. Although it didn't make her feel any better or safer, at least she knew they were around.

Once while Mom was attending early morning prayer at a particular church, she told a few of the men there she was being followed and the men were at the church. The pastor and several of the men stood around the wall and began praying. They made the furry bears so uncomfortable that they left.

Whew, Mom thanked God she didn't see them again until she joined a certain church and guess what; one of them was an usher, but he didn't stay long.

After a while, it became a cat-and-mouse game with them, but then God spoke. God told Mom, "Not a hair on your head will be touched; and it's not what you see, but it's what you don't see."

Wow! What a word; such assurance and consolation. The tables had been turned and now when Mom would see them, they became unsettled.

Mom was driving down Moselle Street when all of a sudden she saw them in her rearview mirror. She quickly swerved to the right, allowing them to pass, and then she got behind them. As they approached Genesee Street, Mom saw them look back at her and almost lose control of their car. Mom could see them struggling to keep their car from going out of control.

Another time, while driving down Genesee Street, one of them was in front of her. He looked back and saw her. Suddenly he turned down Goodyear Street and pulled to the side and just sat there like he had seen something.

Mom was walking behind one of the furry bears at the Galleria Mall when all of a sudden, he threw up his hands and said, "Whew! What's that?"

He turned around, looked at her, stopped walking, and bent over the rails as she passed by.

Mom didn't say a word. She don't know what hit him, but something did.

Another time when Mom was driving, she spotted them first so she began following them. They sped up and she sped up, then God said, "Don't do that." She turned and went down another street, she never saw them again.

Six

WHAT DOES MY MOM MEANS TO ME!

My mom has the strength of an eagle and she is the wind beneath my wings. In her wings lies leadership and in her wings lies a backbone that as an eagle, the dark clouds did rise in her life, and the strong winds did blow,

-But-

My mom mounted up her wings with prayer and God was the only one that brought her through sixty years of her life, even though my father had passed away years ago.

It was God who equipped her and gave her the backbone to make hasty decisions, and in tough situations to carry on hard tasks.

It was God who was on her side, which makes all the difference in the world; and for that, I am proud to say thank you Mom and I love you for the inspiration of the Holy Ghost leading and guiding you in your life.

Love Jetaun

July 2000

This poem was written and read at Mom's sixtieth surprise birthday party

Mom and Dad's Wedding Day

Mom and Dad

The Family

The Matriarch and her Children

Seven

ONGOING REVELATIONS

God has spoken to Mom many times and He continues to speak to her. He often reveals Himself in open visions while she is awake and there are other times while she's asleep. If she were an artist, she could paint some of the most beautiful things He shows her. Whenever she reads the word, He constantly reveals new revelations to her.

She often wonders why God chose her: unlearned, uneducated, doesn't speak well, and can't remember much. However, she can remember every scripture, dream, and revelation that God has ever shown her. You can wake Mom up at any time and all the things that God has put inside of her just flows out of her. HALLELUJAH.

Mom always says, "I'm nothing special at all, just humbled that a GREAT BIG GOD way up there would have time for little old me way down here."

After Dad died, Mom began walking in Delaware Park crying and talking to her daddy; that's who God is to her. Mom recalls telling an old friend about God. Her friend said to her, "You talk about God like He's real." Mom replied to her, "He's real to me." Mom didn't realize she was establishing a relationship, the best relationship she ever had.

Years later after Dad died, one night in a dream, Mom said Dad came to her. He said, "There is something I need to tell you; I was with you too and you didn't know." He said, "Tell Janice I am real proud of her. Keep up the good work," and then he went on to say, "I'm in torment." Mom began to cry and told him, "I don't want to know. I forgive you for whatever it was," and then he went away.

Whatever Dad did, he did it to himself. He could have told Mom before he died. Mom loved him and would have forgiven him. Mom believes the spirit of a person never dies.

God had been with Mom for two-and-a-half years, teaching, instructing, and guiding her. One day, He told her, "I'm going to leave you now, but I'm going to give you something." She was heart-broken and began to cry, as she didn't want Him to leave her because everybody else had always left her. He said, "I'm going to give you the Comforter and you are going to walk and talk for Me and I'm going to use you for a vessel to do My work."

Mom had no clue of the things God was speaking of. In her small mind and limited thinking, she asked God, "Am I going to walk like George Jefferson? You know who that is from *the Jeffersons* on TV?" She is so glad God has a sense of humor and He knew what she didn't know or understand. To be very honest,

Mom still doesn't know or understand why God constantly says or shows her these spiritual things.

Now, some of the things He shows her are not always nice.

Once God said, "Let Me show you something." She was so excited she couldn't wait to see what it was. Mom asked, "What is it?" There appeared two round holes directly in front of her. Imagine looking through a pair of binoculars. He said, "Look through here."

When she looked through the holes, OH MY GOD! It was awful; in a flash, every horrible thing you can imagine appeared. She felt like somebody had hit her in the stomach. It hurt so badly and as quickly as He showed her these things, He took it away.

Mom was sad and said to God, "You always show me nice things, why did You show me that?" He responded, "I wanted you to see what I see all the time."

One night while sleeping, Mom dreamed she was walking in Delaware Park when she saw this lion coming toward her. The expressway was on one side and she knew she couldn't outrun the lion. Mom asked God, "What should I do?" God said, "Speak in tongues." When she began speaking in tongues, the lion laid down.

The next day, Mom went walking in Delaware Park when she saw this man walking toward her. When he reached her, he began walking beside her. God said, "He's a rapist." She asked, "What should I do?" He said, "Start speaking in tongues."

Mom began speaking in tongues and that man began walking so fast, he walked right out of his shoes and right out of sight.

Another day, a little round, black, fuzzy thing with red eyes had been following Mom around the house for about three days. Everywhere she went in the house, this thing would be there. No one else could see it, thank goodness.

While standing in Mom's bedroom talking to her, she began telling me about this thing. I asked her, "Is it standing beside you right now?" She replied, "Yes." "Is it a dog or cat?" "No, it's a little round, black, fuzzy thing with red eyes."

I said to Mom, "I tell you what I'm going to do. We're going to pray so let's go into the living room." As we proceeded into the living room, Mom said the little, black, round fuzzy thing with red eyes didn't follow us. Mom sat on the couch and I sat on the floor at her feet and began praying.

Mom said that thing started walking and walked through the walls, through the doors, out of the house, and to the end of the driveway. It looked left and right, and then took off running toward Genesee Street. Mom said, "I see it running; it's running, and running, until it ran right out of sight."

Mom saw an open field of sticks, but God told her that those were not sticks; "These are My people who have no hope, no faith, and are spiritually dead, and the open field is the world."

Then God told her to look again and then He asked, "What do you see?" She replied, "I see an ocean of water that is dirty and muddy." He said, "Those that reject me are like the restless sea which is never still. They are always crumbling up mire and mud, and there is no peace in God for them."

And then God spoke again; this time His voice was like thunder and He put emphasis on "CONSECRATE YOURSELF! CONSECRATE YOURSELF! The anointing destroys the yoke."

Then He said to Mom, "Tell them that I AM has sent you." She replied, "I don't know anyone by that name." He said, "I AM the Father, the Son, and the Holy Spirit, and when you get there you are going to represent Me."

Mom told God, "Those are some awfully big shoes to walk in." He said, "It won't be you, but it will be the Holy Ghost wrapped up in you."

Then God showed her a hand full of keys. He told her, "I have given you the keys to the kingdom, and you have access at will. Whatever you bind on earth is bound in heaven, and whatever is loose on earth is loose in heaven."

Matthew 16:19

Our family was a member of a particular church when God spoke and told mom to take her family and RUN. "And when you get to the place, I will be there." She remembers saying to God, "I just got here." Mom didn't want to leave, but she was obedient. So every Sunday, our family went visiting from church to church.

31

We found this particular church that we all liked, but God said, "No, they need discipline." WHAT? Boy, that was hard.

Finally, God spoke and called a certain pastor by name. Mom had to admit that she didn't want to go there and we didn't either, but again she was obedient. When Mom got there, she joined and when the pastor stuck out his hand to shake her hand, another hand came out of his robe. She knew it was God's hand. Then God told her to get baptized again, and she did. Mom had been baptized as a child, but obviously that didn't mean anything to God.

Once in a dream, there was chaos everywhere. People were running all over the place, but Mom was running in a different direction with her children, and her arms were stretched out surrounding us. One of my aunts was on the sideline, yelling to her, "You're going the wrong way!" But something in Mom's belly kept telling her to keep running.

We ran and ran until we couldn't run anymore. We fell on the ground from exhaustion. When we stopped, Mom looked around; there was no one. Mom said, "God, where are You?" When she turned all the way around, there stood six white horses and a chariot, and she heard a voice say, "Step on board and take your place."

Mom gathered all her children on that chariot; she put her hands on the reins, and those six white horses took off and ascended into the heavens. She didn't bother to look back, because there was nothing to look back for.

Whenever Mom felt low in her spirit, or just needed a hug from her daddy, she would ask God to give her a song; she needed a song to sing.

"My hope is built on nothing less than Jesus blood and righteousness; On Christ the solid rock I stand; all other ground is sinking sand."

Written by (Mote, Edward 1834) Public Domain

I stand on your word, I stand on your promise, and you promised to never leave me nor forsake me, I need another song to sing.

How Great Thou Art
Written by (Hine, Stuart K. 1953)
Publisher (Hine, Stuart Trust CIO)

Mom remembers another time when God asked her if she had faith the size of a mustard seed. She answered, "Surely I got that much. I'm a country girl." Then He told her to stay on the straight and narrow path; don't get too far left or too far right.

Then He said to her, "I will continue to guide you and keep you healthy too, and you will be like a well-watered garden and overflowing springs."

And then God took her to the scripture of Isaiah 58:11:

"And the Lord shall guide thee continually, and sat-
isfy thy soul in drought, and make fat thy bones;
and thou shalt be like a watered garden, and like a
spring of water, whose waters fail not."

Another time, Mom experienced being absent from her body.
She wondered if she was dead. She was in a white place, very com-
fortable and beautiful.

Initially, Mom didn't see anyone and wondered where she was.
She saw all the old prophets walking around in their robes, looking
good. What an experience.

God once took Mom above the sky. It's difficult to explain this
in any other words. Think of being in an airplane in the sky at the
highest altitude. He took her above that, and then He showed her
the most magnificent, splendid, and awesome wonders. He pulled
back the curtains and showed her the band of angels. Mom told
God, "I can get used to this."

Once Mom saw Jesus walking on the water. There were six
people standing on the right dressed in white, but there was a man
standing behind them.

The man looked like her grandson Greg, but she couldn't say
for sure. This man began falling back, but Jesus reached over the
other people, grabbed that man, and stood him up strong. Whoever
that man was, he will never fall.

34

One Sunday morning, God told Mom to go to a specific family member's house, and He said this time talk not pray, so she went. After about thirty minutes of them just talking, mom stood up to leave when she heard in her spirit "seventy-two hours, things are going to turn around." Mom told her what she had just heard. She responded, "When it happens, I'll let you know."

Monday came, Tuesday came, and God bless Wednesday. The family member called Mom and asked, "Are you sitting down?" She began telling Mom that she received a check for sixty-thousand dollars; money she was expecting that Mom had no prior knowledge of and they never discussed until after she received it.

After they rejoiced about the move of God, the family member stated she wanted to start her own business, and again Mom heard in her spirit, "Tell her to pursue." Mom told her.

As Mom visits different churches, she prays for the people on the sick list. God spoke and said, "I desire to heal many of My people, but many of My people don't have the faith to believe that I can do it."

A cleaning woman praying in a rich man's house is another account of an awesome God and the Holy Spirit.

Mom often worked as a cleaning woman doing light cleaning and dusting in the evenings, but make no mistake about it; mom never had to work and she would be quick to let you know that. She would say Honey; see that NFTA bus out there? That takes care of Artie Hunt this little money is just chump change.

Well one evening Mom arrived at this particular house to do her routine light cleaning and dusting when the wife of the house told Mom that her husband was not feeling well and to not worry about cleaning upstairs. That's when the Holy Spirit spoke and told Mom, "Pray for him." Mom responded, "What do You want me to pray for him for? He has everything: he's rich, he's white, and he's Jewish."

By this time, the wife was coming downstairs and Mom met her at the bottom of the stairs and told her, "I have to pray for your husband." She replied, "I don't think so." Mom responded, "Oh I know so," and she began to pray.

The wife clasped her hands together and afterwards, she said, "I can believe for my husband and children, but I can't believe for myself."

After the prayer, God said, "Ask him how many years does he want." Mom said to God, "You mean to tell me You want me to pray for this man and ask him how many years he wants," but she didn't ask.

Immediately after the prayer, the husband came down those stairs, went into his office, and worked until Mom left. Days later, his secretary came to Mom and asked, "Have you heard? They took him to the doctor and they couldn't find anything wrong with him."

Another time, one night, an angel came to Mom and said, "Let's go; I'm taking you somewhere." They walked through doors and then arrived at the house of this particular person. They walked up the stairs into his bedroom, where he was sleeping.

The angel touched the bottom of his feet, and he sat up and looked startled. Something came out of Mom and went back into this individual stomach.

She could see the movement in his pajamas; it made four moves as it settled inside of him and then it stopped. The angel said to her, "You're going to be alright now," and then she woke up.

One Sunday after attending church, Mom came home and laid across her bed. In a vision, she saw a snake crawl through our dining room window. When she approached the snake, it coiled up. Mom said to the snake, "You are not going to bite me." The snake then turned into an individual that was a member of that church.

Another time, while Mom was in Sunday school at that same church, there was a woman teaching. As she was speaking, Mom saw something come up out of the woman's mouth and spray the congregation, and then go back down in her.

Before Janice (me) was fired from her job, God gave Mom this word "dismantled" and then He said "safe." Neither one of us knew what the meaning behind it meant. We were hoping that after whatever was going to be dismantled, I would be safe. That was not the case.

A short time later after I was fired, God spoke to Mom again and this is what He said, "Dismantled did not come from me but I allowed it to happen. I add and multiply; I never subtract or divide, and since I allowed it to happen, I'm going to give them a black eye for doing it." I'm still waiting on that black eye.

One day, God told Mom to go to Tops and get some olive oil. She couldn't believe God knew we have a Tops supermarket. Mom heard Him, but she ignored Him.

A few days later, God asked in a harsh voice, "Where is the oil?" You should have seen Mom; she backed that car out of the driveway and couldn't get to Tops fast enough. Once she got there, frantically she asked, "Where is the oil?" Someone directed her to the aisle.

Mom finally returned home with the oil, then she asked God, "What do I do now?" He said, "Pray over it!" The only prayer she knew at that time was Psalm 23 and the Lord's Prayer, so she repeated that. Then God said, "Anoint yourself!" Well, Mom was a Baptist girl and she didn't know anything about oil or anointing herself.

Then He said, "Pour it on you!" She didn't know exactly what that meant, so she just took the oil and made an x on her forehead. You're talking about hilarious. As Mom think back about that now, she laughs.

On November 2, 2017, Mom had this dream about being under clear water. She got out of the water and then back in. She could see under the water, and she wasn't afraid and didn't drown. Everything was peaceful and calm. So she went to scripture.

Revelation 3:5:

"He that overcometh, the same shall be clothed in white raiment; and I will not blot out his name out of the book of life, but I will confess his name before

my Father, and before his angels."

Mom understood this to represent the Book of Life. It represents God's record of those who are part of His kingdom. The Book of Life contains a record of all those who accept Jesus Christ as Savior and who will receive eternal life. "That's me, Artie, Praise the Lord. River of Life." Then the angel showed her the river of the water of life; it was clear as crystal. Some think the flowing water refers to the Holy Spirit, others to the promise of eternal life, and still others to the abundant life that God gave to His people. Probably, all of these ideas are included in this symbol. Praise God mom received this for herself.

Whatever the detail, this picture is one of indescribable beauty and glory. Eternal life means a whole new dimension of living. There will be people with new life, purpose, and action. God is the focus of this city and the source of light and everything else.

God's spectacular glory illuminates the city, as is illustrated by the lack of night. His presence fills the whole city, making the need for a temple obsolete. The New Jerusalem itself is a temple filled with the glory of God.

Eternal life will be pure, untainted by evil. In the New Jerusalem, we can escape not only the power and penalty of sin, but also the presence of sin.

God is still revealing Himself. God is a good God, yes He is! A song from the Holy Spirit.

Mom always call God her friend. "What a friend we have in Jesus, all our sins and grieves to bear, what a privilege it is to carry, everything to God in prayer."

Written by (Converse, Charles Crozat 1855)

Public Domain

In past times, Mom desired to have a relationship with her siblings. She thought by doing things for them that would make them closer, and then one day God spoke to her and said, "Enough is enough. After you do all that, it's going to be business as usual. You can't make nobody love you or accept you. Go on and don't look back." Mom asked God, "Am I that bad of a person?" and God said, "It's not about you," and then she burst into tears and that was the end of that.

There is not a day that goes by that Mom doesn't express how grateful she is for God and her children. She often tells us she doesn't know what she would do without us.

The number seven represents completion, and all the things that have been shared with you up to this point are **COMPLETE**!

Eight

WHO I AM

⟨⟨♥⟩⟩

The number eight represents a new beginning, Mom's new beginning; no longer questioning, "Who Am I," but knowing, "Who she is." She went from believing to knowing, and this is what she knows.

Colossians 2:10:

"And ye are complete in him, which is the head of all principality and power."

First Peter 2:9:

But ye are a chosen generation, a royal priesthood, an holy nation, a peculiar person that ye should shew forth the praises of him who hath called you out of darkness into his marvelous light.

First Peter 1:23:

"Being born again, not of corruptible seed, but of incorruptible, by the word of God, which liveth and abideth forever."

Second Corinthians 5:17:

"Therefore if any man be in Christ, he is a new creature; old things are passed away; behold, all things are become new."

John 5:24:

"Verily, verily, I say unto you, He that hearth my word, and believeth on him that sent me, hath everlasting life, and shall not come into condemnation: but is passed from death unto life."

Romans 8:1

"There is therefore now no condemnation to them which are in Christ Jesus, who walk not after the flesh, but after the Spirit."

Psalm 1: 1-3:

"Blessed is the man that walketh not in the counsel of the ungodly, nor standeth in the way of sinners, nor sitteth in the seat of the scornful.

But his delight is in the law of the Lord; and his law doth he meditate day and night. And he shall be like a tree planted by the rivers of water, that bringeth forth his fruit in his season; his leaf also shall not wither, and whatsoever he doeth shall prosper."

Galatians 2:20:

"I am crucified with Christ: nevertheless I live; yet not I, but Christ liveth in me: and the life which I now live in the flesh I live by the faith of the Son of God, who loved me, and gave himself for me."

Psalm 23:

"The Lord is my shepherd; I shall not want. He maketh me to lie down in green pastures: he leadeth me beside the still waters.

He restoreth my soul: he leadeth me in the paths of righteousness for his name's sake.

Yea, though I walk through the valley of the shadow of death, I will fear no evil: for thou art with me; thy rod and they staff they comfort me.

43

Thou preparest a table before me in the presence of mine enemies: thou anointest my head with oil; my cup runneth over.

Surely goodness and mercy shall follow me all the days of my life: and I will dwell in the house of the Lord forever."

Self and Group Assessment
Let's Have A Conversation

1. Do you believe there is a God? Why or why not?

2. Does prayer help? Yes, No, Sometimes

3. Have you ever questioned your faith or the faith of others? If so, why?

4. Have you experienced any of the same struggles? If so, how did you handle them?

5. Discuss what you've read. Does it question you to think differently about what you believe?

6. Which chapters stand out for you and why?

7. Are these accounts believable to you? Why or why not?

8. Through the eyes of Jetaun, what does the poem say about her mother's experiences and their relationship?

9. What are some of your experiences and the relationship you have with your mother?

10. What are some of the things you struggle with and how do you address them?

11. After reading this book, what are your thoughts about life?

12. Discuss your personal feelings about Prayer, Faith, and Guts.

OTHER INSPIRING
BOOKS TO READ

The Bible	All Versions
I Found A Good Man	Jean Baldon Harris
Destined For Greatness	Angel C. Davis
The Private Life Of A Public Woman	Rhonda D. Henderson
Broken Into Pieces	Karen Anderson Hardaway
God Did It	Dianna Hobbs
Changing Your Past To Protect Your Future	LaToya N. Williams

HOPE
How Faith Carried Me
Through My Darkest Hours

Mercedes E. Wilson

Strategic Prayer

Eddie Smith and
Michael L. Hennen

Regaining Vision

Mickey Freed

Prayer Warrior

Stormie Omartian

His Passionate Pursuit

Victoria Boyson

Super Saints

Kathleen Steele Tolleson

About the Author

Janice Marie Hunt

Orator, Facilitator, Mentor, Teacher, and Author

Passionate, Powerful, and Practical

Motivational and Inspirational

Passion For What I Do And

Compassion For The People I Do It For

Driven To Providing A Realistic

And Positive Change

Janice has an Associate of Science Degree in Business and a Bachelor of Business Administration Degree from Medaille College, Buffalo, New York.

Currently, Janice is teaching the Fundamentals of Public Speaking at Medaille College.

Isaiah 50:4:

"The Lord God hath given me the tongue of

the learned, that I should know how to speak a

PRAYER, FAITH, and GUTS *Determined To Make It!*

word in season to him that is weary: he wakeneth

morning by morning, he wakeneth mine ear to hear

as the learned."

To contact Janice Marie Hunt for speaking engagements, email
msjanicemariehunt@gmail.com